NATIONAL GEOGRAPHIC

Ladders

Golden Gate Bridge

AMERICAN WONDERS

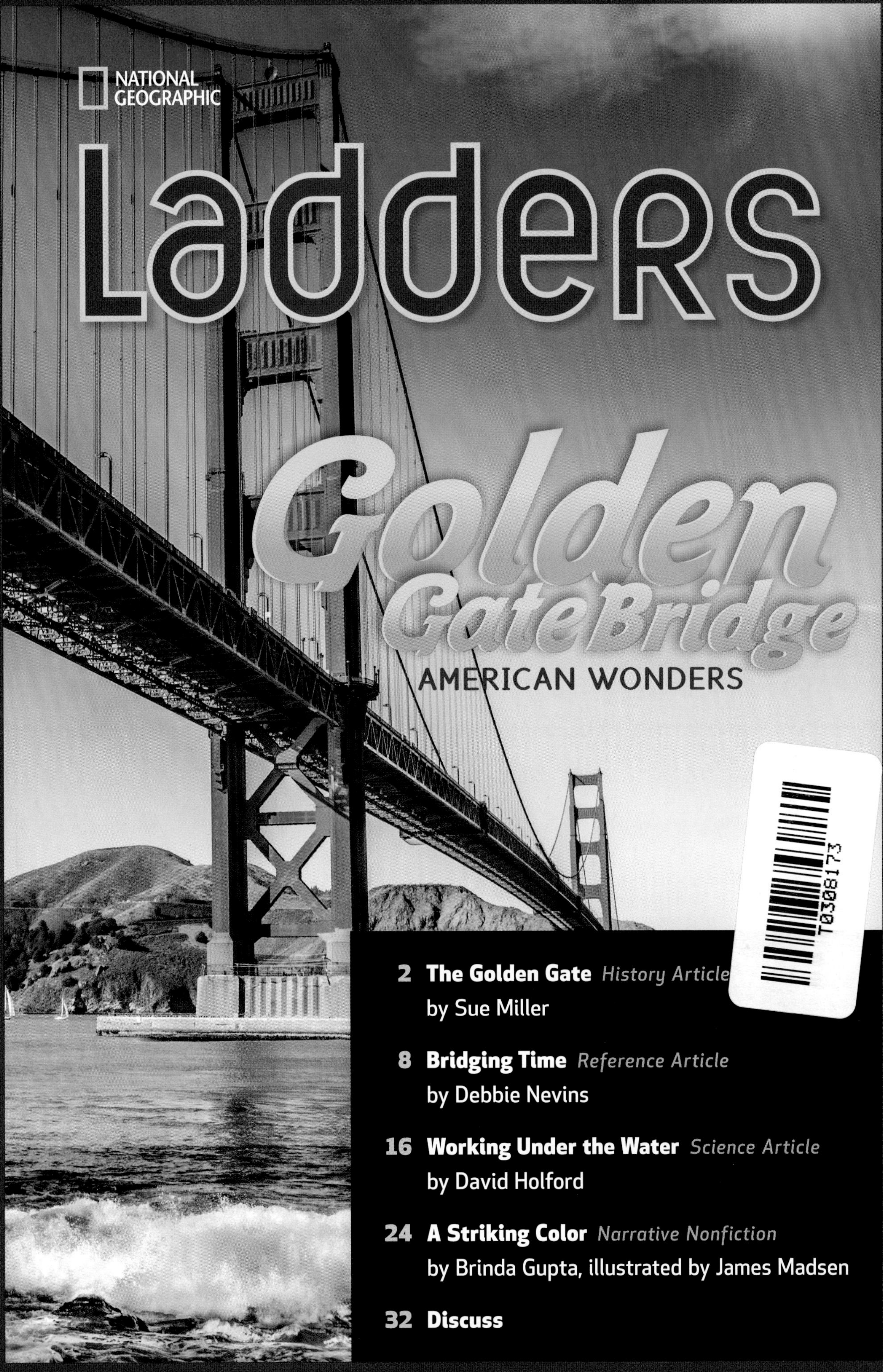

GENRE History Article

Read to find out why and how the Golden Gate Bridge was constructed.

The Golden Gate

by Sue Miller

The Golden Gate Bridge stretches across the Golden Gate Strait.

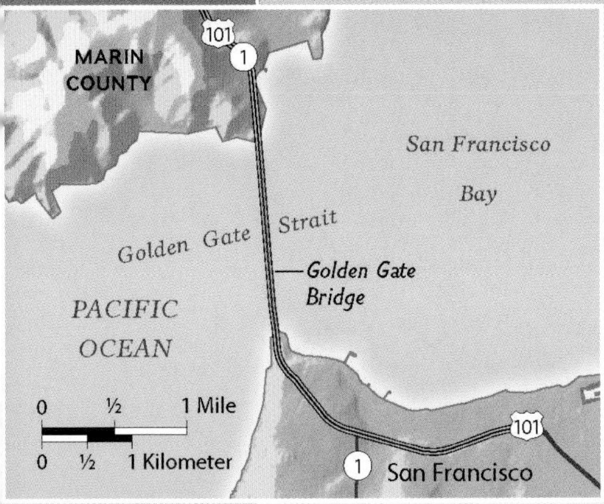

The Golden Gate Bridge connects the city of San Francisco with Marin County.

The waters may look calm in the picture below, but the Golden Gate **Strait** is well known for rough seas and thick fog. The Golden Gate Strait is a large waterway that connects the Pacific Ocean and San Francisco Bay. It is also the northern border of San Francisco, California.

In northern California, the Golden Gate Strait separates the city of San Francisco from Marin County. In the 1900s, many people from Marin

County worked in San Francisco. So in 1919, San Francisco city officials asked if it was possible to build a bridge across the strait. At the time, riding a ferryboat was the only way between San Francisco and Marin County.

Expert after expert said no to the bridge idea. They claimed that earthquakes, heavy fog, high winds, deep water, and **riptides** would make building a bridge too difficult. A riptide is a strong current that flows from the shore toward the ocean. Riptides make underwater construction, which is necessary for building bridges, very difficult and dangerous.

Bridge engineer Joseph Strauss proved them all wrong. He believed he could build a bridge across the strait. His final design was a **suspension bridge**. It would use overhead cables to support the roadway high above the water, so that boats could pass under it. The mayor and the public welcomed Strauss's ideas. However, the ferryboat owners were not excited about the bridge. Fewer people would use the ferries to cross the strait.

Celebrations and Dangers

February 26, 1933, was a day of celebration. At least 100,000 people gathered to watch the official groundbreaking ceremony that marked the start of the construction of the Golden Gate Bridge. Navy planes flew overhead. Hundreds of pigeons were released into the sky. There were speeches and a parade. Only a lucky few were close enough to clearly watch as San Francisco's mayor and another official used a shiny golden shovel to break ground where the bridge would be built.

At the time of the ceremony, work on the bridge had actually already begun. On January 5, 1933, people were hard at work laying the base for the huge towers that would hold the bridge's main cables in place. The main cables would stretch from tower to tower. A series of smaller cables hanging from the two main cables would attach to the roadway, holding it up.

By the end of that year, work on the towers had begun. The north tower was the first one built, followed by the south tower. Both rise 746 feet into the sky.

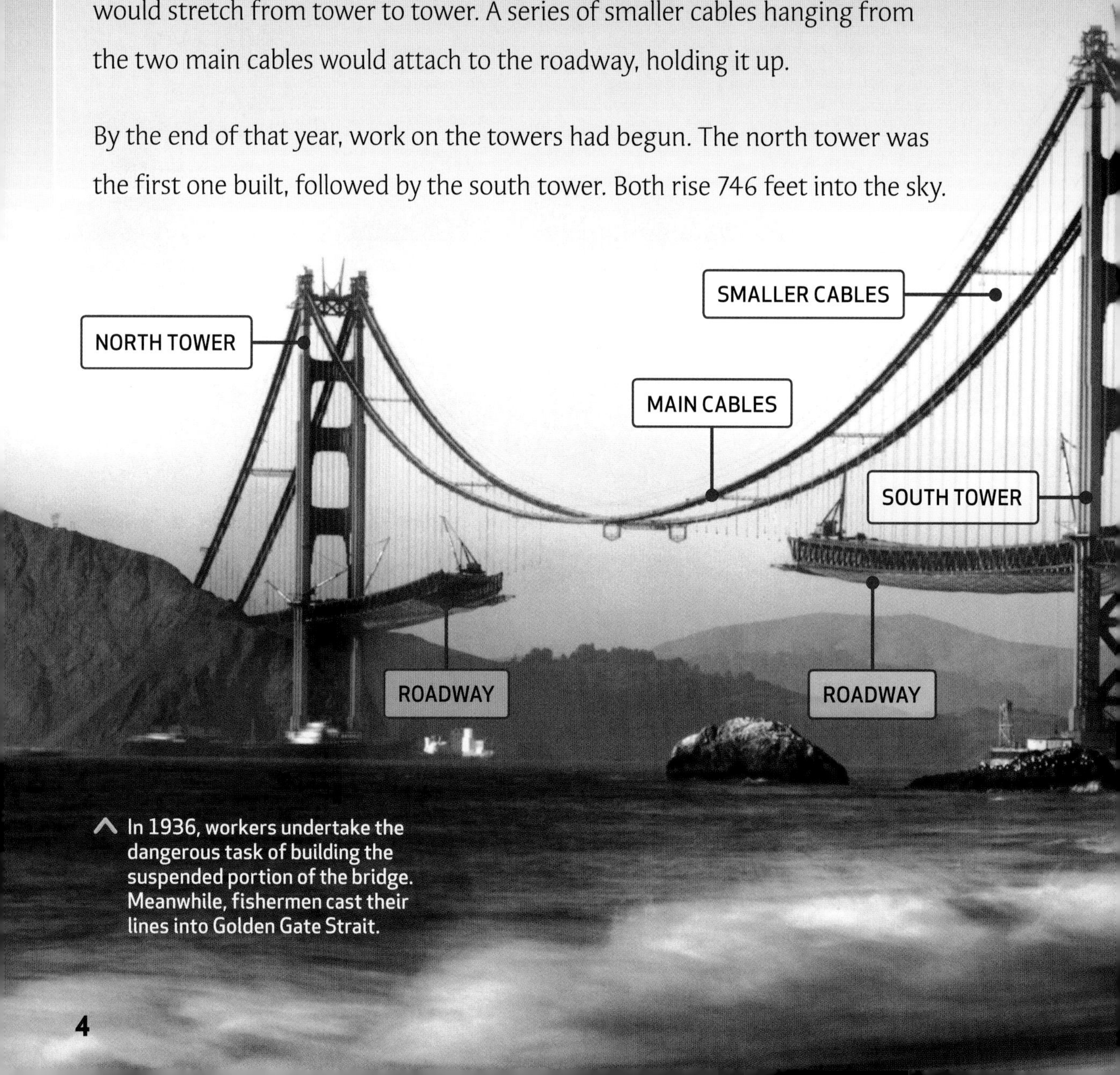

^ In 1936, workers undertake the dangerous task of building the suspended portion of the bridge. Meanwhile, fishermen cast their lines into Golden Gate Strait.

Workers had to spin and string the main cables from tower to tower.

Workers had to brave wind, weather, and heights to **weld** about 600,000 rivets, or bolts, into each tower. Welding is the process of using heat to melt metal so it joins together.

Once both towers were complete, the cable spinning began. Workers used a wire-spinning machine to turn 80,000 miles of thin steel wire into strong, flexible cables. Once all of the cables were in place, workers began building the suspended roadway. Teams worked at both ends of the bridge. They met in the middle and completed the roadway by April 1937. To mark that day, Edward Stanley—the worker who drove the first rivet into the bridge—tried to hammer in a golden rivet, only to have the unheated metal smash to pieces. But that was only a minor accident, and it couldn't distract the workers from the pride they felt over the great work they had done. In a little over four years, at a cost of around $35 million, they had made Strauss's impossible task a reality.

The First Ones to Cross

Finishing the Golden Gate Bridge was a proud moment for the city and for the country. The people responded by throwing a huge party! In May 1937, they came from near and far to celebrate a whole week of festivities.

On the first day of the celebration, the public was invited to cross the brand-new bridge on foot. Imagine what it must have been like to be one of those people. In all, about 200,000 people walked, ran, roller-skated, walked on stilts, rode unicycles, and even tap-danced across the bridge that day. Nearby, city officials held a formal ceremony following a parade full of

Golden Gate Bridge opened to foot traffic on the morning of May 27, 1937. Thousands of people were already waiting to walk across it.

floats and marching bands. The next day, the bridge opened to cars. More than 32,000 cars and almost 20,000 people paid the small fee, or toll, to cross the bridge.

The people of San Francisco had every right to celebrate. The Golden Gate Bridge would connect the city to the rest of the country much better than ferries ever could. This helped the region grow in size and wealth. Even today, the bridge is one of the most famous symbols of San Francisco, drawing tourists from around the world.

This postcard is from the late 1930s. It shows many of the famous sights that San Francisco offers visitors.

Check In What kinds of challenges did workers face as they built the Golden Gate Bridge?

GENRE Reference Article

Read to find out about the history of the Golden Gate Bridge.

Bridge Time

by Debbie Nevins

THE GOLDEN GATE BRIDGE IS ONE OF THE NATION'S MOST BELOVED LANDMARKS FOR GOOD REASON. IT HAS WEATHERED STORMS AND EARTHQUAKES AND SERVED AN IMPORTANT ROLE FOR PEOPLE, INCLUDING COMMUTERS, PROTESTERS—EVEN BUNGEE JUMPERS! IN FACT, MORE THAN A BILLION CARS HAVE CROSSED THE BRIDGE SINCE IT OPENED IN 1938. FOLLOW THE BRIDGE CABLE TO READ THIS TIME LINE AND LEARN ABOUT THE EXCITING HISTORY OF THIS AMERICAN WONDER.

1924

It's a go! A telegram message to San Francisco's mayor announces that the Golden Gate Bridge project has been approved by the U.S. government.

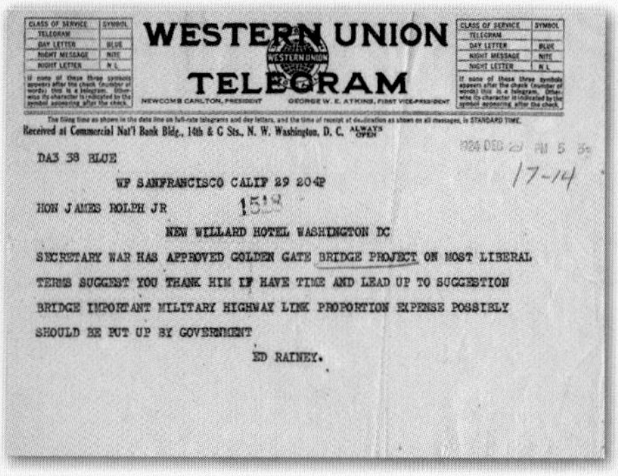

WESTERN UNION TELEGRAM

NEWCOMB CARLTON, PRESIDENT   GEORGE W. E. ATKINS, FIRST VICE-PRESIDENT

Received at Commercial Nat'l Bank Bldg., 14th & G Sts., N. W. Washington, D. C. ALWAYS OPEN

DA3 38 BLUE

WF SANFRANCISCO CALIF 29 204P

HON JAMES ROLPH JR

NEW WILLARD HOTEL WASHINGTON DC

SECRETARY WAR HAS APPROVED GOLDEN GATE BRIDGE PROJECT ON MOST LIBERAL TERMS SUGGEST YOU THANK HIM IF HAVE TIME AND LEAD UP TO SUGGESTION BRIDGE IMPORTANT MILITARY HIGHWAY LINK PROPORTION EXPENSE POSSIBLY SHOULD BE PUT UP BY GOVERNMENT

ED RAINEY.

1933

Construction of the bridge begins, and it won't be easy. Workers will struggle against strong tides, frequent storms, and fog. Eleven men will die building the bridge.

In August, a fog-bound steamship hits a **trestle**, or support, causing great damage.

1934

A federal prison opens on Alcatraz Island in San Francisco Bay, east of where the bridge is being built. The harsh prison is said to be escape-proof, or impossible to escape, but a few prisoners will try. Some of the nation's most dangerous criminals will "do time" here.

NG

1937

In March, famed pilot Amelia Earhart flies westward over the still-unfinished bridge in a small plane called a Lockheed Electra. It's the first part of her attempt at a round-the-world flight. This attempt will not succeed. Later that year, she will try again. Unfortunately, her plane will disappear over the Pacific Ocean.

Opening Day! On May 27, San Francisco Mayor Angelo Rossi cuts through a chain, opening the bridge on "Pedestrian Day." Some 200,000 people stroll on the bridge. The following day, the bridge opens to automobile traffic.

1935

The spinning of the bridge's main cables begins. Each of the two cables will be 7,650 feet long with 27,572 steel wires inside. They will take more than six months to spin.

1938

In October, Blackie, a 12-year-old horse, wins a $1,000 bet for his trainer. Blackie swims across the Golden Gate Strait in 23 minutes, 15 seconds, beating two human challengers. The trainer, Shorty Roberts, who couldn't swim, holds on to Blackie's tail the whole way!

1942

Ghost ship passing? Crew members onboard the Navy ship USS *Kennison* report seeing the **phantom** SS *Tennessee* going under the bridge. They say the spooky ship left a trail of churning water to mark its path, but there are two troubling things about their story. First, radar, a machine that detects moving objects at a distance, found no trace of the phantom ship. Second, the *Tennessee* crashed and sank in these foggy waters back in 1853!

1955

TV fitness celebrity, Jack LaLanne, age 41, swims from Alcatraz Island to the shore of San Francisco—handcuffed!

1957

Rock and roll! A 5.3-magnitude earthquake strikes just south of San Francisco, causing a huge amount of damage to the city. Fortunately, the bridge was designed to be flexible in heavy winds and earthquakes. The bridge twists and turns, but it isn't damaged.

1958

It's a boy! The first baby is born on the bridge. In the 1990s, two more babies—both boys—will also be welcomed to the world on the bridge.

1959

Fog is a common condition on the bridge. In May, a movie crew tries to film a scene of the make-believe destruction of San Francisco. When the 15-person crew sets up on the bridge early in the morning, it's so foggy, they can't see a thing. By the time the fog lifts, it is rush hour and the filming causes a huge traffic jam.

1963

Reversible lanes are added to the bridge, allowing some lanes to change direction depending on what time of day it is. This helps ease traffic jams on the bridge during rush hours.

1968

The Golden Gate becomes the first bridge to charge one-way tolls. Drivers traveling south into the city of San Francisco pay a 50-cent toll, but those traveling north to Marin County cross for free. This arrangement helps ease traffic jams, in one direction at least. Today the southbound toll is $6.

1972

The Golden Gate National Recreation Area is established as a national park. Some 80,000 acres of open land on both sides of the bridge are preserved for the public's **recreation** and enjoyment.

1985

The one-billionth car crosses the bridge.

1987

To celebrate its 50th anniversary, the bridge closes to automobile traffic in the morning. Just like "Pedestrian Day" in 1937, "Bridgewalk '87" gives people a chance to cross the bridge on foot without worrying about car traffic. That day, about 300,000 people rush onto the roadway.

1993

In March, five young men try to bungee jump from the bridge. Bridge authorities arrest them for trespassing, or entering the area without permission. Over the years, other people will bungee jump, illegally and unnoticed, from the bridge. But the official rule remains, "No jumping, bungee or otherwise."

1994

The American Society of Civil Engineers names the Golden Gate Bridge one of the Seven Wonders of the Modern World.

1996

The bridge is a popular place to express opinions about world problems. In November, protesters take to the bridge to oppose the chopping down of redwood trees in northern California.

1998

The United States Postal Service issues a special stamp to honor the Golden Gate Bridge.

2000

The largest crane in the world, floating on a barge, squeaks under the bridge with only 13 feet to spare.

2001

In the middle of the night, pranksters hang a car off the side of the bridge. Mystified bridge workers cut the cable and let the car fall into the water. Engineering students from Canada admit to pulling this stunt.

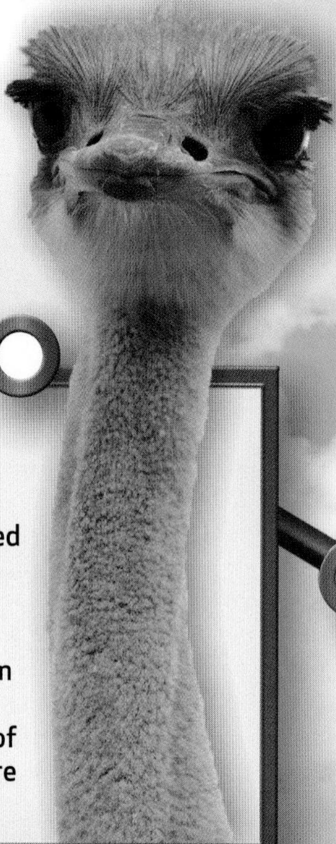

2005

Big bird on the loose! While being transported across the bridge, an ostrich escapes from the back of a minivan. The bird runs around on the road for about 10 minutes at the height of rush-hour traffic before being captured.

2007

On November 18, artist and San Francisco resident Michael Grbich celebrates his 75th birthday by tap-dancing across the bridge.

2009

You can walk, run, or drive over this bridge, but you cannot ride a horse. In May, one man and his horse find out the hard way when the California Highway Patrol forces them to turn around and leave.

2010

In April, the Harlem Globetrotters, famous for their comedy and basketball skills, dribble and pass their way across the bridge.

2012

On September 21, the space shuttle *Endeavor* flies over the bridge in an official farewell. Piggybacked on a 747 jet, the retired craft is headed to the California Science Center in Los Angeles for display.

2011

In August, the Hershey Company builds a model of the Golden Gate Bridge out of candy.

On October 21, people across the country join First Lady Michelle Obama in an attempt to break the Guinness World Record for doing the most jumping jacks in a 24-hour period. One group does its jumping jacks on the bridge. It's all part of Mrs. Obama's "Let's Move" campaign.

2013

Electronic toll-taking makes it faster and easier to cross the Golden Gate Bridge than humans collecting the fees. Cameras read cars' license plates as they cross, and drivers receive bills for their tolls.

2012

Happy birthday Golden Gate! The bridge is 75 years old and festivities celebrate its history, beauty, and engineering brilliance. Scientists install solar "birthday candles" on its spires.

Check In Which of these events on the bridge would you like to have seen? Why?

GENRE Science Article

Read to find out how workers build underwater.

Working Under the Water

by David Holford

The Golden Gate Strait is one of the world's most dangerous bodies of water. Here, in this narrow strait, water from the Pacific Ocean surges into San Francisco Bay. At the same time, water from the rivers that flow into the bay pushes out. This clash produces violent **currents** that flow in many directions. These difficult water conditions caused many people to believe that it would be impossible to build a bridge over the strait. Workers would have to do part of the work in the water.

However, **commercial divers**, people who are paid to work underwater, took on these underwater challenges and dangers. It took skill, bravery, and special equipment to build the awe-inspiring Golden Gate Bridge. Many divers felt honored to be a part of one of the United States' largest construction projects ever.

"My part in building the bridge was to plant explosive charges that blew up rocks to prepare the ocean bottom," says one diver. "I had to guide 40-ton steel panels lowered by cranes into position on the bottom," recalls another. Other workers removed tons of loose earth after explosions. They also smoothed the muddy bottom of the Golden Gate Strait using high-pressure hoses. Some workers welded pieces of steel together to form the base of the bridge. All of this happened deep underwater.

The oval-shaped structure in the middle of the strait was created to build the tower's base. Then water was pumped out of the oval. This left a dry area to work in.

Divers only had four 20-minute sessions each day to work under the water. They had to be out of the water when currents were stronger and more dangerous.

Workers used cranes to remove rock and earth loosened by underwater explosions. They cleared the ocean bottom to make room to build the base of the bridge.

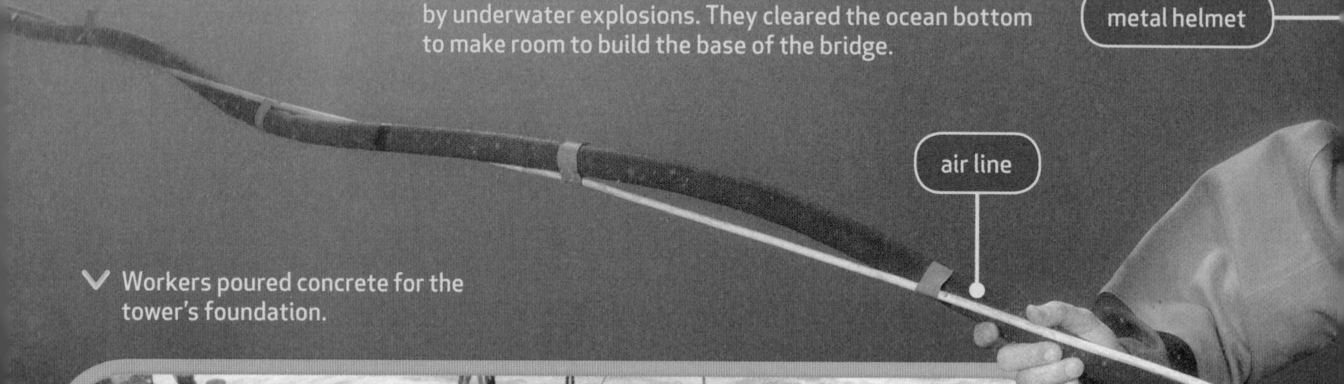

Workers poured concrete for the tower's foundation.

The Bridge That Divers Built

Stretching across the wide strait, the Golden Gate Bridge hangs gracefully from thick steel cables attached to two enormous towers. One tower sits on the shore. Its base is firmly planted into the ground. The other tower is different. It rises high out of the water, held upright by a concrete **foundation**, or base, deep underwater on the ocean floor.

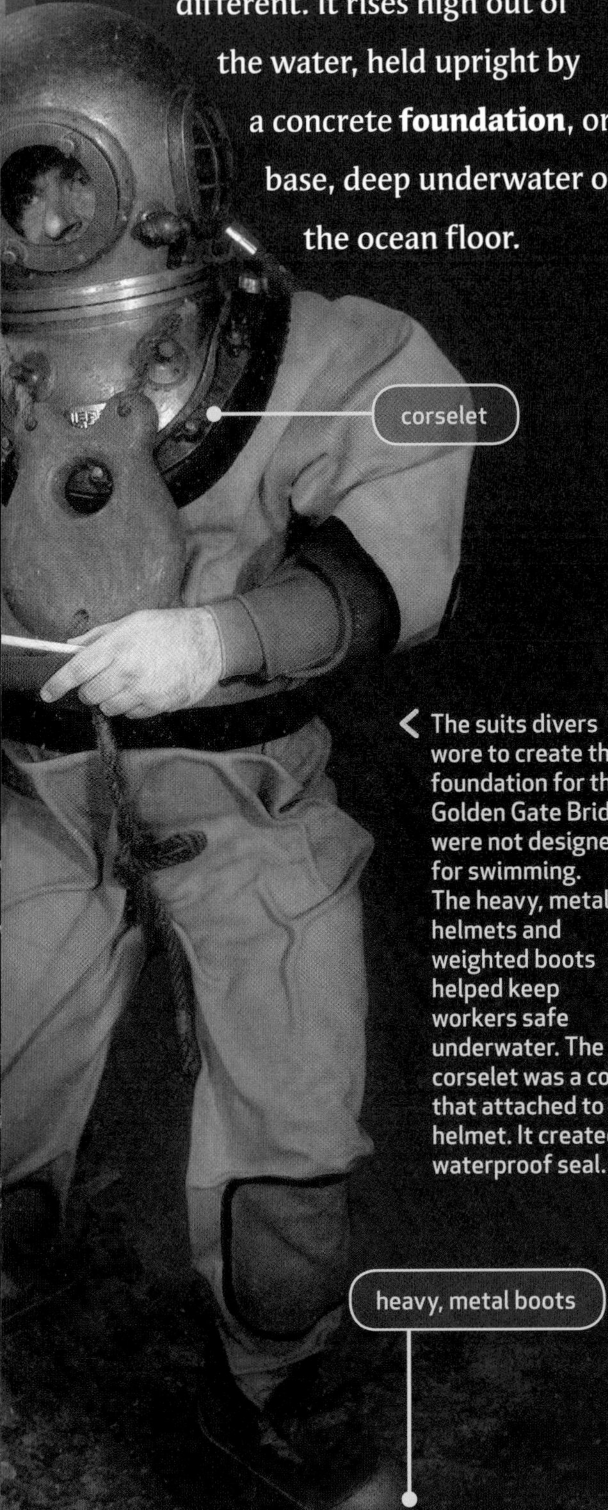

The suits divers wore to create the foundation for the Golden Gate Bridge were not designed for swimming. The heavy, metal helmets and weighted boots helped keep workers safe underwater. The corselet was a collar that attached to the helmet. It created a waterproof seal.

To begin bridge construction, workers first had to blast away the underwater rock on the bottom of the San Francisco Strait. This made space for a strong, level foundation for the bridge's tower. When the floor was smooth and clear, they began constructing an oval-shaped wall on the strait floor. It surrounded an area the size of a football field and extended above the water. Once the wall was complete, workers pumped millions of gallons of water from the center. This left a dry, empty space in the middle of the strait. Now they could build the cement foundation of the tower here without getting wet.

With the water gone, workers filled the inside dry area with cement and allowed it to harden. Then water was pumped back into the structure. Water was now on both sides of the wall. As a result, pressure from the strong currents wouldn't destroy the structure.

Back under the water, divers positioned steel beams into a framework to create the tower. The steel framework reached above the waterline, high into the air. Now the rest of the bridge could be completed above the water.

Different Dives and Duties

The divers who built the Golden Gate Bridge were not diving in order to have fun. When we think of divers today, we usually think of rubber-suited swimmers gliding past colorful fish in the ocean. However, commercial divers enter the water to work. Their duties range from replacing underwater pipes in rivers to inspecting walls that prevent floods for damage caused by a hurricane. On any given day, commercial divers may use tools such as drills, sledgehammers, and torches to repair an oil rig out in the middle of the ocean. They might even rescue an old sunken ship and its treasure from far offshore.

Sometimes divers work in swamps, harbors, or even sewers that carry waste water through underground pipes throughout cities. These divers often can't see what they are doing because the water is too dark and murky. They must be able to stay calm in this black environment. They need to feel their way around to build or repair something. Can you imagine fixing underwater equipment that you can't see? In these situations, divers attach a cable to their suit. Following the cable helps them find their way back to the surface.

The proper tool is very important to commercial divers. This diver is using a tool to secure bolts.

This diver is writing notes underwater. He uses a special pad and writing instrument that works in water.

Keeping the Bridges Strong

Divers around the world help build new underwater structures such as bridges, dams, and canals. They also maintain, or keep up, structures that were built 20, 40, or even 100 years ago. This includes the Golden Gate Bridge. Some underwater workers dive deep into San Francisco Bay to patch cracks in the underwater tower's foundation. Others work underwater to strengthen the tower so it can better withstand California's frequent earthquakes.

Modern divers face the same challenges and dangers in the Golden Gate Strait that divers faced years ago when they built the bridge. Strong currents, cold, murky water, and heavy diving suits made for difficult working conditions for the divers who built the bridge.

Dive suit technology has improved. That has made it a little easier for divers to work underwater. However, the other factors remain the same. Still, thanks to the bravery and skill of these divers and the underwater workers who maintain the bridge today, the Golden Gate Bridge continues to stand, as strong and stable as ever. It is an example of American imagination, courage, and skill.

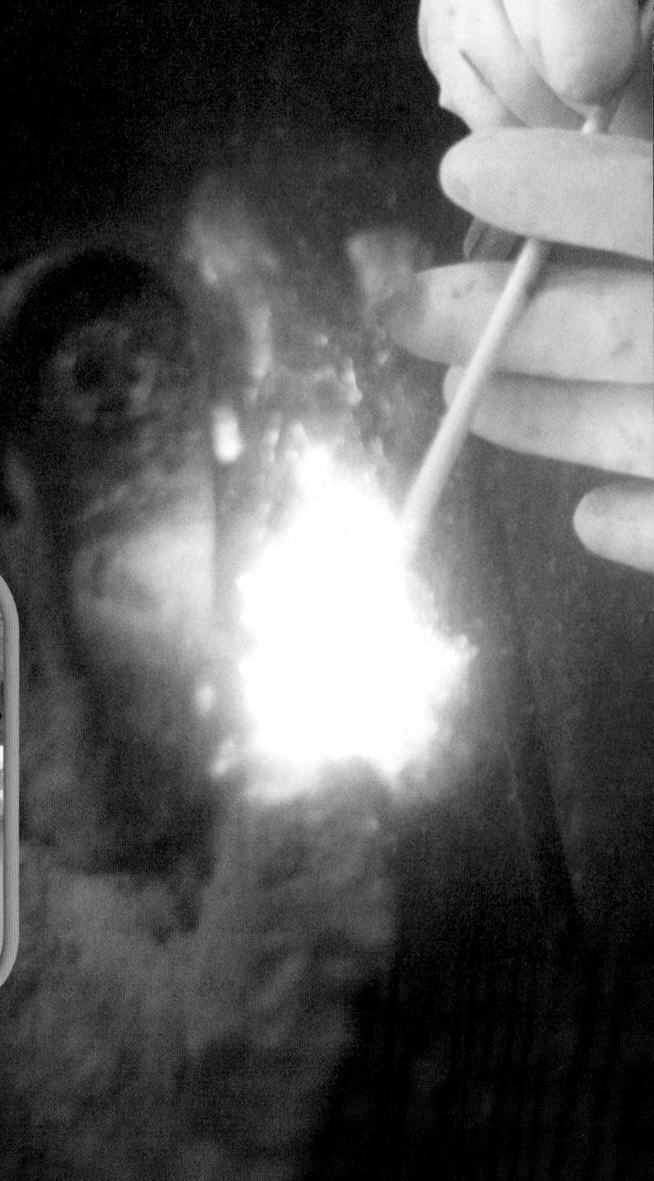

^ Some divers wear dive masks instead of helmets, depending on the job they have to do.

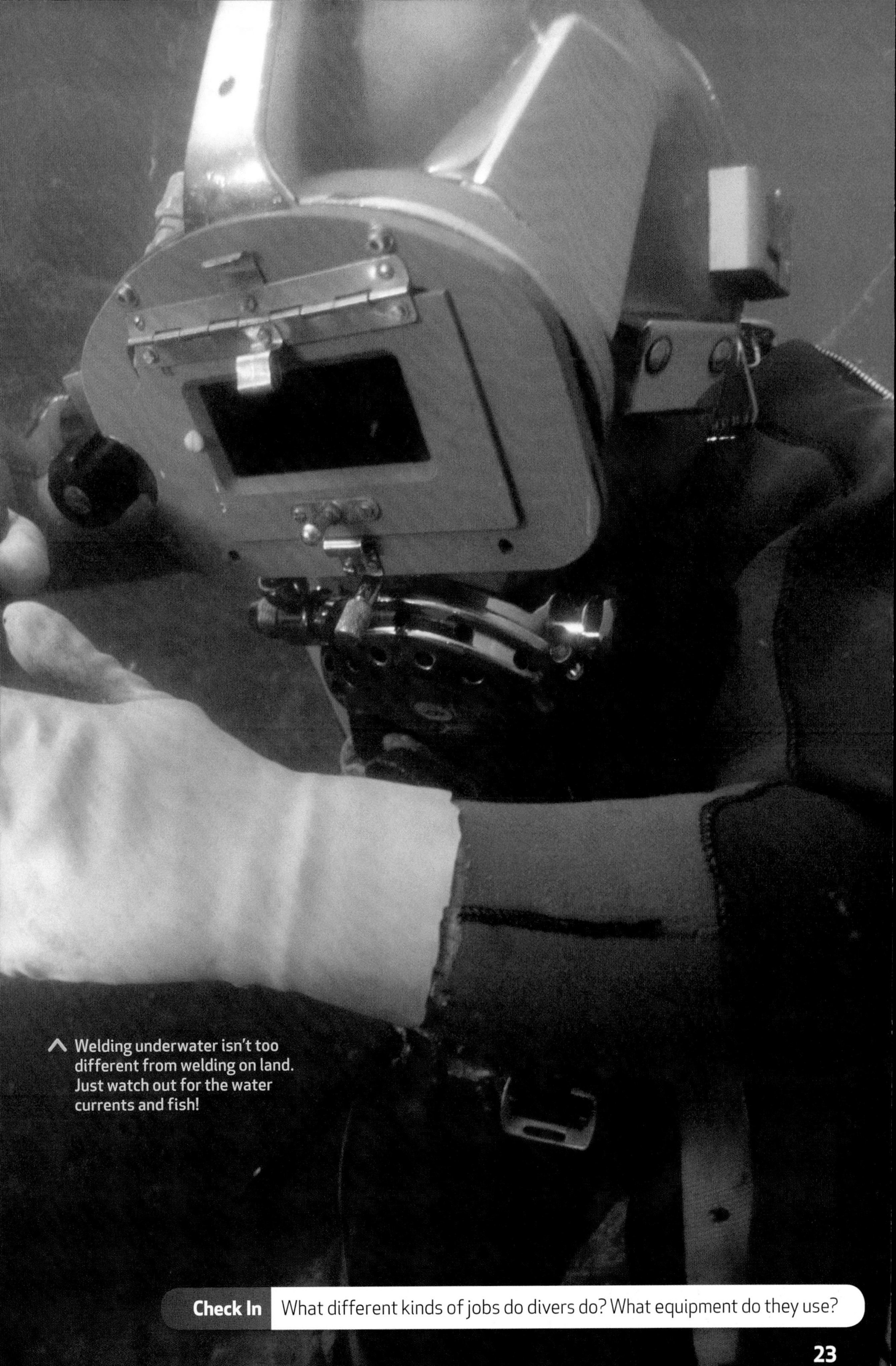

Welding underwater isn't too different from welding on land. Just watch out for the water currents and fish!

Check In What different kinds of jobs do divers do? What equipment do they use?

GENRE Narrative Nonfiction

Read to find out how the Golden Gate Bridge got its unique color.

A STRIKING COLOR

by Brinda Gupta illustrated by James Madsen

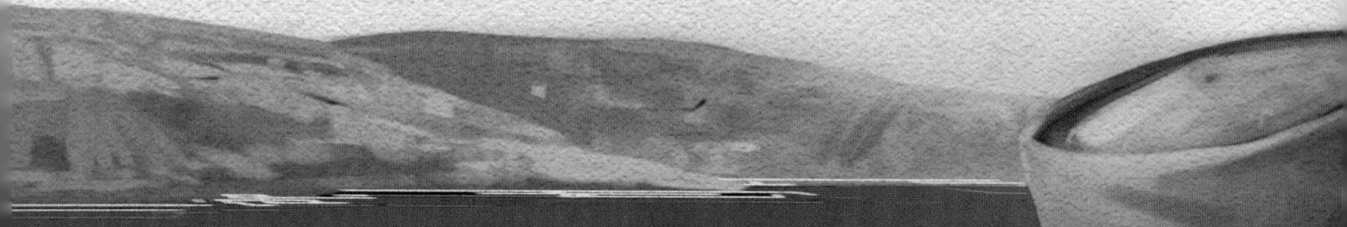

You're standing in the Presidio, a park on the northern tip of San Francisco. The *Golden Gate Bridge* soars almost over your head. Although the structure is a human-made marvel, it somehow fits in with the peaceful views of nature around you—the gold and green of the hills surrounding the bay and the gray of the fog drifting down from the sky. The bridge's bright color contrasts nicely with the blue of the water and sky. However, the bridge's color has nothing to do with its name. In fact, the name *Golden Gate Bridge* was in place before the color was chosen. Why isn't this bridge a metal gray, like so many others?

Workers taking the ferry between San Francisco and the towns in Marin County in the 1930s were lucky. Not only could they look at beautiful scenery on their trip from home to work and back, they also had a daily view of busy workers building the Golden Gate Bridge.

Bridge architect Irving F. Morrow stood on the ferry deck during his commute to the construction site. His fellow passengers watched as he examined the bridge from different angles and made sketches in his notebook. From the ferry, Morrow observed the bridge in different kinds of light and different kinds of weather. He had already drafted a great design, but he knew he still had important decisions to make. Most bridges were black, gray, or silver. It was likely that the steel Golden Gate Bridge would be, too. But as Morrow sketched, he wondered—maybe this special bridge should be different.

With the help of other architects, engineers, and artists, Morrow studied how different colors looked against the water and the hills. He thought of all the questions he knew the public would ask him:

Should the bridge stand out, showing off its modern design?
Or should it blend into the scenery that people already enjoy?
What colors would look good against the colors of the water and hills?
What colors would stand out in San Francisco's frequent fog?

"Black is an obvious choice for a bridge," said some people.

Morrow colored his sketches black and thought,
"That's ugly. And it makes the bridge look small."

"Silver is an easy color to maintain," said others.

Looking at his sketches, Morrow said, "Silver makes the bridge look like an airship."

The U.S. Navy was worried about ships seeing the bridge in dense fog. Would Morrow consider eye-catching black and yellow stripes?

"Absolutely not!" said Morrow. "Stripes would look ridiculous."

"This bridge is special," Morrow reminded himself. "It will be important for transportation, but that's not all. It sits in some of the prettiest scenery in the world. It will be a symbol for San Francisco, for California, and even for the United States. It can't be ordinary in any way."

Morrow found an extraordinary color, although its name wasn't very creative. The color, called International Orange, was a bright reddish orange. Morrow saw this bright orange color marked on some of the steel used to build the bridge, and he thought it was perfect.

Bridge officials were startled. Orange? The color seemed wild and strange. Wouldn't it spoil the landscape? People might complain that it hurt their eyes to look at it. It wasn't the safe, proper color that they had imagined.

"The Golden Gate Bridge is one of the greatest monuments of all time," Morrow reminded them. "Its color shouldn't be safe."

Everyone reluctantly agreed . . . and soon, they realized they had made the right choice. International Orange certainly stood out. It stood out to ships navigating the water in heavy fog. It stood out to tourists admiring the view from far away. But the rich color also blended well with the colors of the bridge's surroundings. International Orange looked great against the blue sea, the green and gold hills, and the many colors of the San Francisco skyline.

Morrow had picked a color that showed off the magic of the bridge. It also allowed the bridge to become part of the Bay Area's natural beauty.

Over time this once-unusual choice of color became quite popular. People around the world started requesting International Orange so they could use the paint color in their homes and on their cars and bicycles. It's a specially mixed color just for the bridge, but the city of San Francisco includes the color's formula on its Web site, so paint stores can make it. Now people can create whatever they like using the exact same color of International Orange.

FRESHENING THE COLOR

From that first coat of paint in 1937, San Franciscans and people around the world love the orange color of this unforgettable bridge. It is a color that fits San Francisco perfectly. But keeping the paint bright is a full-time job.

Painters must climb almost 750 feet high. They paint every inch of the bridge.

Because of the area's salt water and fog, the paint wears away quickly. Luckily, the layers of paint protect the steel underneath from salty air, rust, and **corrosion**, or the wearing away of metal. A crew of about 30 workers maintains the bridge's paint. They touch up worn spots all week. Although they stop painting when it rains, they still paint in heavy fog and wind. Since the painters have close-up views of the bridge, they tell other crews when the bridge needs repairs.

To keep the bridge looking fresh at all times, the crew uses 5,000 to 10,000 gallons of paint a year. About 20 years ago, the paint **manufacturer** changed its formula to make the paint fumes safer to breathe. That, plus improved safety equipment, helps the Golden Gate painters during their days of hard work. Because of them, visitors to the bridge can see Morrow's exact vision at any time of the day or year.

Check In Why did Morrow choose International Orange? What other options did he consider?

Discuss

1. What connections can you make among the four selections that you read in this book? How are the selections related?

2. What would it have been like to be one of the first people to cross the Golden Gate Bridge on "Pedestrian Day"? Use the descriptions of the sights, sounds, and feelings that the author included to describe what those first pedestrians must have experienced.

3. Why were the waters of the Golden Gate Strait especially dangerous for the divers building the Golden Gate Bridge?

4. Summarize the sequence of events that led to the decision to paint the Golden Gate Bridge International Orange.

5. What do you still want to know about the Golden Gate Bridge? How can you find out more?